A Truett Cathy

IT'S BETTER TO BUILD BOYS THAN MEND MEN

S. TRUETT CATHY

FOUNDER OF

Chick-fil-A

WITH DICK PARKER

LOOKING GLASS BOOKS

Also by S. Truett Cathy

It's Easier to Succeed Than to Fail

Eat Mor Chikin: Inspire More People

The Generosity Factor
  with Ken Blanchard

Published by Looking Glass Books
Decatur, Georgia

Printed in the United States of America
ISBN 1-929619-20-0

CONTENTS

A good child nearby is about to make bad choices that will have lasting consequences and needs for you to step in right now.

This book is for that child.

My hope is that by reading about the experiences of some children I have known, you will be inspired to reach out to a child near you—a child full of potential who needs the guiding hand of a wise adult.

FOREWORD

By Art Linkletter

My friend Truett Cathy is one of the extraordinary people of my generation. Our shared commitment to children and our crusade for creating positive role models for children has made our friendship significant for me.

We have both striven to be positive role models ourselves. And we have both shared a philosophy for honesty and fair dealing in our professional and business lives. That is why I feel honored by his request for this foreword.

During the past thirty years I have devoted my life to helping young people grow up under difficult conditions to be God-loving, fairminded, caring people. Never before in the history of Western civilization has a generation of children been subjected to such an avalanche of vulgarity, violence, drug abuse, and sexual promiscuity.

Raising a family is life's greatest challenge. When we reach out and influence a child for good, it is perhaps the most important thing we will do in a lifetime. Yet, parents in America spend less time with their children than in any other country in the world. Almost 2 million children aged seven to thirteen take care of themselves until one of their parents comes home from work.

I will never forget the gasp from my TV audience when I asked a six-year-old boy what he'd take to Heaven if he had his choice. He replied, "My mother and dad, because I think they would have more time for me up there."

Our children are the living messages we send into a time we shall not see. And I would hope that parents will find great truths and much encouragement in Truett's book.

I bless him for writing it.

Art Linkletter, radio and television star for more than sixty years, is author if Kids Say the Darndest Things *and twenty-five other books. He has served on the Presidential Advisory Council for Drug Abuse Prevention, the Presidential Commission to Improve Reading in the U.S., and the Presidential Commission on Fitness and Physical Education.*

Chapter One

CHANGING A CHILD CHANGES YOU

*"Whoever welcomes one of these little children
in my name welcomes me."*
—Mark 9:37

God wants to work through you to change the life of a child.

He will provide the love, the encouragement, the joy, and the hope. All you have to contribute are arms for hugs, a voice to encourage or to discipline, and time for companionship.

You don't have to look far to find the child. In fact, your paths will probably cross this week. And when you reach out, your reward will be immeasurable. Every child God touches through you will be changed, even if you don't see the transformation with your own eyes. And you will be changed by every child God touches through you.

I was thirteen years old when God worked through Theo Abby, my Sunday school teacher, to change my life.

In a real sense, I had been "fatherless."

My father was alive. In fact, he was home every night, and I never knew him to gamble or drink or cheat on my mother. But he never told me, "I love you." And when I needed help, like the time when I was sick on a rainy Sunday morning and had to get my newspapers delivered, I knew not to even ask him. As I grew toward manhood, my father and I never discussed the difficult issues of life.

Then Theo Abby became my teacher and my friend. Occasionally he visited the federal housing project where I lived to see me and other boys in our class, and he invited us to go with him and his son Ted to his lakeside cabin. There he modeled with Ted a loving father-son relationship.

As an adult I remembered Mr. Abby's example and decided to teach boys in Sunday school. Like Mr. Abby,

I kept in touch with the boys through the week by inviting the entire class to be my guests at the Dwarf House, my first restaurant, one night a week. I soon began to see how children bursting with potential can wither on the vine without adequate guidance from adults.

Eleven-year-old Harry Brown, whose quiet demeanor reminded me of myself as a child, had a father like mine, distant and hard to please. When Mr. Brown abandoned the family altogether, Mrs. Brown was left alone to bring up five boys. She did a remarkable job, and I tried to give Harry special attention in class or during our weekly dinners. I set goals for my class in their Bible reading, and Harry met every one. His mother and I encouraged him at every step.

Then my wife, Jeannette, and I moved from the neighborhood, and I didn't see Harry for more than twenty years. By the time we met again, he and his wife, Brenda, had become foster parents, providing the fatherly love and two-parent stability for others that Harry had missed as a teenager.

God blessed us with the opportunity to see Harry blessing others.

When Jeannette and I were led by God to build foster homes, Harry retired from Southern Bell so that he

11

Children all around us are growing up without strong positive guidance from their parents, who are busy, distracted, absent, or who choose to be buddies instead of parents to their children.

and Brenda could become houseparents. Twenty years into "retirement," they are still raising children twelve at a time at our WinShape Homes.

God worked an incredible transformation in Harry's life, and He blessed me with the opportunity to see Harry now blessing others.

Children all around us are growing up without strong positive guidance from their parents, who are busy, distracted, absent, or choose to be buddies instead of parents to their children. You see these boys and girls playing with your children or grandchildren, or in your church, or in your classroom or Scout troop. They're a bit quieter or a bit more rambunctious or a bit different from the other children. You may know about trouble in their homes—divorce or the death of a parent or grandparent. Or, like my friend Kevin, they may be in a stable, two-parent home.

THE CHILD OF A BUSY MAN

"My father was a busy person," Kevin says. "He didn't spend a lot of time with me."

Today Kevin is in jail. In fact, he's spent more than half of his adult life behind bars as society attempts to mend him.

The Result of Fatherlessness

The United States is the world's leader in fatherless homes. The results of our actions, according to the Fathers' Manifesto:

63% of youth suicides are from fatherless homes.

90% of all homeless and runaway children are from fatherless homes.

80% of rapists motivated with displaced angers come from fatherless homes.

71% of all high school dropouts come from fatherless homes.

85% of youth in prisons grew up in fatherless homes.

75% of all adolescent patients in drug treatment centers come from fatherless homes.

Children from Fatherless Homes Are:

5 times more likely to commit suicide

32 times more likely to run away

20 times more likely to have behavioral disorders

14 times more likely to commit rape

9 times more likely to drop out of school

10 times more likely to abuse chemical substances

9 times more likely to end up in a state-operated institution

20 times more likely to end up in prison

Meanwhile, Kevin's son has grown up spending even less time with a father than Kevin did. As a result, Kevin says, "He's a chip off the old block. When he was eight years old he got off the school bus and went down the street taking mail out of mailboxes. He took the envelopes home and opened them up to see if there was anything of value there."

Don't be too concerned that your children don't listen to you. But be very concerned that they see everything you do.

Ten years later, when Kevin's son was eighteen, he had already been in and out of jail just like his father. If Kevin's son has a son, the odds are he will follow the pattern set by his father and grandfather before him. And if you think their situation is unusual, you're not looking around.

So why did Kevin, whose father was "a busy person," and Harry, whose father abandoned him, turn out so vastly different? I haven't found any simple answers, but I have seen one pattern. Every child I know who overcame long odds and grew into a responsible adult can point to an adult who stepped into his or her life as a friend, a mentor, and a guide.

We are all, as Kevin described his son, chips off the old block. If parents are not trustworthy, they should not expect their children to be trustworthy. Parents who gamble or drink can expect their children to do the same. I often remind parents, "Don't be too concerned that your children don't listen to you. But be very concerned that they see everything you do." And I tell my thirteen-year-old Sunday school boys, "If you give your parents trouble, you can count on your children giving you trouble."

A child needs a new model to break the generational cycle, an adult who will show him or her a better way. For some children that better way will be a new way of thinking, and they will need continual positive reinforcement. My prayer is that this book will give you the inspiration and the tools to walk alongside children who need a guiding hand at the critical moments in their young lives. Why don't you join Harry Brown and me in following Theo Abby's model? It's simpler than you might think.

I will share some of the lessons I have learned as a dad, a foster granddad, and a Sunday school teacher for nearly fifty years, along with thoughts from foster home houseparents, from Chick-fil-A restaurant Operators who work directly with dozens of young people every day, and from Jeannette, who grew up in a home without a father and relied on her heavenly Father from the age of five.

Every idea that works has its basis in Scripture. Many of the lessons in this book come from Proverbs 22, from which I drew my life verse seventy years ago: "A good name is rather to be chosen than great riches, and loving favour rather than silver and gold" (Proverbs 22:1, KJV).

That chapter in Proverbs also includes the timeless reminder, "Train a child in the way he should go, and when he is old he will not turn from it" (Proverbs 22:6).

> *The best thing you can do to help a child is follow your instinct and God's leading.*

Additionally, Proverbs 22 offers advice on common sense, generosity, control of your temper, hard work, quality work, sexual abstinence, money management, corporal punishment, and trust in the Lord, among other things.

I hope the thoughts and illustrations in this book help you in particular situations, but the best thing you can do to help a child is follow your instinct and God's leading. Reach out to children sincerely. Reach out in love. Love children into a sense of belonging. Let a child know you care and you're available to talk—to be a friend. Encourage children honestly, reminding them of their strengths and their opportunities. There are no magic words. All you can do is share a bit of yourself, allow God to use you to plant a seed in a child, and pray that it takes root.

Chapter Two

RESPECT

Train a child in the way he should go,
and when he is old he will not turn from it.
                                    —*Proverbs 22:6*

Disciplining children in an undisciplined society may be the hardest task parents face. I'm going to make it even harder by suggesting that you should discipline children who are not your own.

Doug and Julie Bowling were twenty-three years old when they became houseparents at our second foster home. One day they were a typical young couple with an infant son; the next day they had seven children ranging in ages up to fifteen. Julie recalls the first supper she served: "I worked for two hours getting it ready and called them in when I had it on the table. As soon as they finished eating, they all got up at once and ran outside to their bikes and skateboards, leaving dishes everywhere.

"Doug and I looked at each other and realized that wouldn't do, so we went to the front door and yelled, 'Get back in here!'

"They filed back in, and we explained to them, 'This is not camp, and we're not your counselors.' From that moment we began to define our relationship."

The Bowlings had initially suggested that the children call them Doug and Julie. After all, they certainly weren't old enough to be the children's biological parents. "Mom and Dad" sounded weird to them. Then came Doug's trip to the emergency room with their eight-year-old boy. The doctor couldn't understand the relationship between the child and the man he called Doug and wasn't sure Doug had authority to sign a medical release. Finally Doug convinced the doctor that he was the boy's foster father.

"This is not camp, and we're not your counselors."

"From now on," he told the children when he returned home, "you're calling us Mom and Dad."

Children Don't Need Extra Buddies

Children have plenty of buddies. They don't need an adult—especially a parent—to be another buddy. They need someone they can look up to with respect. That respect begins with the establishment of authority. God emphasized the point with the first three of the Ten Commandments:

You shall have no other gods before me.

You shall not make for yourself an idol.

You shall not misuse the name of the Lord your God.

Then, in the fifth commandment, He told us who is next in line after Him:

Honor your father and your mother.

Although it is often said, it bears repeating: Children want limits, and they want to be able to respect the adults who set those limits.

Establishment of authority begins with the name you are called. For Doug and Julie and their new foster children, it was Mom and Dad. I like for our foster children to call me Grandpa. You may want children outside your family to call you Mr. Jackson or Mrs. Daniels or Coach or Pastor. In less formal situations they might address you as Miss Katherine or Dr. Tommy. In the

South children sometimes call close friends of their parents Aunt Jane or Uncle Greg, even though they are not related. All of these titles imply the authority adults should have in the eyes of children, and in almost every case they're more appropriate than a simple first-name basis.

Several of our houseparents coach Little League baseball, basketball, or soccer, and most of them have two basic rules for their team. Players must say "Yes sir" to the coach and do whatever he asks them to do. Players cannot laugh at another child who makes a mistake. A couple of our dads have even told parents of disrespectful children, "I don't want your child talking to you that way around our team. They're setting a bad example." Respect begins with the way we speak to one another.

Although it is often said, it bears repeating: Children want limits, and they want to be able to respect the adults who set those limits. They want to know where the fence is; that's their security. And, finally, they want to know what will happen when they cross the line. A parent who tries to be a buddy will soon have a tyrant for a child. The same theory applies in any adult-child relationship. Our houseparents establish their authority with each child by being firm, knowing they can always ease up at the appropriate time. If they begin the relationship by being lax, they have a hard time imposing new rules later. That's where the next principle of discipline comes in.

Be So Consistent You're Boring

A child should know, or at least be able to predict, the consequences of any action. Going back to Doug and Julie's house for another illustration, they had been houseparents for a little more than a year, and all of the children knew the rules.

At a family meeting shortly after a new child moved in, Julie told them about something she had planned, and the new boy said, "That sucks."

Instantly the room fell silent, and the other kids turned slowly toward him.

"What? What did I say?" the new boy asked.

The children explained to him that nobody talked like that in their house, and he was in big trouble. Julie and Doug had been so consistent in their discipline that the children knew the consequences by heart.

Contrast that story with David, a boy in my Sunday school class who was having problems getting along with his parents—disobeying them and even making fun of them. I explained to David that when he was being disrespectful to his parents, he was being disrespectful to God. He said he would do better.

A few weeks later I asked David how he was getting along with his parents. He said, "We're working on it."

I said, "You don't need to 'work on it.' You just need to realize who's boss. If you can't take orders from parents, you might not ever be able to hold down a job."

In David's case, I'm afraid the parents never established themselves as leaders of the household through consistent discipline. He would have to rely on a compassionate but firm teacher, coach, or boss to demonstrate consistency.

How many families have you seen that are ruled by a child? By age five, some children already dictate to their parents what they will do.

How many families have you seen that are ruled by a child? By age five, some children already dictate to their parents what they will do. They know their parents would rather give in to their demands than deal with a tantrum.

I've seen dozens of children through the years who never understood respect for authority. Their parents rarely enforced discipline at home until the children were completely out of control, then they flew off the handle and slapped or hit the children. Their inconsistent message only amplified the problem.

Be so consistent with your discipline that you're boring.

A Word about Corporal Punishment

Some parents rely on Proverbs 22:15 to command respect: "Folly is bound up in the heart of a child, but the rod of discipline will drive it far from him."

But the merits of corporal punishment are debatable, and the "rod" does not have to be literal. If you strike a child in anger, you may lose control. My father was that way. If we didn't respect him in every way, he'd pull out the leather strap he used to sharpen his razor and whip us unmercifully. We didn't do anything to cross my dad.

Many of the children who come to our foster homes have been physically abused. They've been thrown against walls and across rooms. They've been slapped hard by angry parents. State regulations prevent physical punishment of foster children, so the houseparents have to be creative in their punishment. For example,

You don't have to be the world's strongest man to earn the respect of a child or a teenager, but you have to be strong enough to stand your ground against an onslaught of resistance.

when the whole house is going out for Chick-fil-A or pizza, a child being punished might have to take a peanut butter sandwich from home. Or you can deny television or computer privileges. A child would rather get a spanking than be denied TV for a week. The most effective punishment isn't always the first one that comes to mind.

Paul Anderson, who was "The World's Strongest Man," built a home in south Georgia for boys who were in repeated trouble and who otherwise would be in youth detention. Those boys knew they couldn't frighten or intimidate Paul Anderson, and by his mere presence he commanded respect. But they learned to respect Paul's heart and his words more than his physical strength.

You don't have to be the world's strongest man to earn the respect of a child or a teenager; you do have to be strong enough to stand your ground against an onslaught of resistance.

The Power of a Rocking Chair

I have relied on the power of a rocking chair hundreds of times since I learned about it more than twenty years ago. We had not yet built our first foster home, and I asked the director of a foster facility near our Chick-fil-A headquarters in Atlanta how she handled discipline.

"If they're misbehaving," she said, "I grab them by the collar, put them in my lap in the rocking chair, and say, 'Let me rock some of the meanness out of you.'"

Now all of our foster homes have rocking chairs. I have "rocked the meanness" out of many infants, young children, and even teenagers who needed to experience quiet, soothing love.

You may think children have outgrown the desire to be rocked to sleep at night. They haven't.

You may think children have outgrown the desire to be rocked to sleep at night. They haven't—particularly children who haven't had an abundance of love expressed to them. They're eager to be rocked or hugged and reminded that they are loved.

So if you don't have a rocking chair, get one. And if you have one, use it.

The Power of Silence

A visit to a church with the WinShape Home family in Brazil showed me the power of silence. After a long service on hard pews, I asked the foster mother,

Christina Stevanato, how they managed to keep the children quiet and still. She said, "They don't have an option." She earned their respect through consistent discipline, and they knew what was expected of them.

I came home and explained to my Sunday school boys that they no longer had an option about whether to behave or to sit quietly through the lesson. If they choose to do otherwise, I briefly stop the lesson, and in the silence of the moment the transgressor realizes what is happening and stops. Of course, the power of silence only works when children respect the person in authority.

Model Respect for Authority

If children have no respect for authority, no amount of punishment is going to change them. One of the best ways to teach children respect for authority is to model our own adherence to the chain of command. Adults can do this by worshiping and respecting God and by obeying the rules of law. It amazes me how many people will cheat on their income taxes, lie to a police officer who stops them for speeding, or take advantage of a clerk who gives them too much change—in clear view of their children. And it saddens me how many families no longer worship together and show their respect for the ultimate Authority.

The first day Alan showed up in my Sunday school class, he was wearing a coat and tie, his shirt was pressed neatly, and his polished shoes gleamed. He raised his hand and answered several questions correctly.

When church started that morning, I noticed that he sat with his mother; his father was not in church. After church, though, Alan's father picked him up in his car and they drove off.

The next week Alan was back, and the scenario repeated itself. Over time I learned that Alan had a close relationship with his father. They were friends. Every Sunday after church they played golf or went hunting or fishing together. The father had simply chosen not to attend church—not to acknowledge a higher Authority through worship. He left it to his wife to take Alan each week.

In addition to being bright, Alan was industrious. He had a paper route and was saving his money to buy a car. By the time he turned sixteen, he had saved enough for a car and a motorcycle, and his parents allowed him to buy them. With the freedom his vehicles gave him, he found a new set of friends, and he no longer came to church. I later learned that he and his father stopped their Sunday afternoon routine as well.

In the summer of 1969, when war and riots were splitting America at the seams, I stood in the driveway at Alan's home and watched his family dissolving. As Alan rode away with his friends in a beat-up Volkswagen van for a music festival in upstate New York, his father asked, "What did I do wrong?" He begged Alan to stay home, but Alan refused.

Soon Alan's girlfriend became pregnant. Any hopes of college had vanished, and a child was born to unwed teenage parents.

His father asked, "What did I do wrong?" He begged Alan to stay home, but Alan refused.

Whether I had an answer for Alan's father on that August afternoon didn't matter. I gave him what I thought he needed, sympathy. But I felt more sympathy for Alan, because in the critical years long before he turned eighteen, something had gone wrong. He needed more direction than he had received; he needed to be shown how to submit to authority. Because he no longer respected his father, he disregarded him at a critical time. When Alan's child arrived, I worried about the home life that little baby would experience—if he would be built up as a responsible young person or mended later as an adult. How would Alan teach him respect for authority?

What's Important Now

The word *win* can stand for "what's important now." One year I challenged the boys in my Sunday school class to be 100 percent on time with their Bibles, prepared for the lesson, and then to stay for church after Sunday school. One morning we were on target to meet the challenge. Everyone was there on time and prepared. The class ended, and we all headed for the sanctuary except Rayburn, who said he was going home. I didn't understand. Rayburn's mother worked in the nursery, and his sister always stayed for church, so it would have been easy for him to stay. The other boys were disappointed, and so was I.

"Rayburn," I said, "you could stay for church if you wanted to, couldn't you?"

"Yes," he said, and he hung his head.

Then I scolded him a bit and reminded him how important it was to the other boys and me to achieve our goal. We were so close to perfection! But Rayburn wouldn't budge, so I sent the other boys on to church.

Then Rayburn pulled me aside and said, "Mr. Cathy,

the reason I have to go home now is to be with my dad. He's there at home, and he gives me his undivided attention while my mother and sisters are gone. He gives that time to me."

"Isn't he there on Saturday?" I asked

"Yes," Rayburn said, "but he's drinking, and there's a lot going on. We don't get much time together. Sunday morning is the only time when it's just me and Dad."

A boy needs time with his father, and a man needs time with his Father. Rayburn's father made the wrong choice. But I told my young friend, "I'm sorry for what I said, Rayburn. You're making the better decision to go home and be with your dad."

BAND-AIDS ON SEVERE WOUNDS

If we choose not to build children with discipline but instead wait until they're adults to "fix" them, the best we can do in many cases is to put a Band-Aid on a severe wound.

My neighbor Lew Rabbit, an airline pilot, dedicated much of his life to applying such Band-Aids. Lew kept a guest house on his property where he invited drunks to come in and dry out. He arranged his flight schedule so he could be home at night, and every night, if he had an empty bed in the guesthouse, Lew drove the streets of downtown Atlanta in search of anyone who wanted to be "mended." It was never easy. The men had to commit to staying for at least thirty days, and they couldn't touch alcohol while they were there. He had many repeat visitors through the years—men who left and picked up the bottle again.

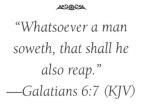

"Whatsoever a man soweth, that shall he also reap."
—Galatians 6:7 (KJV)

"I've never seen a man who didn't fall off the wagon a time or two before he finally got his feet on solid rock," Lew says. Some of the men were never able to find that solid rock. And it all began with a choice each man had made years earlier. It goes back to sowing and reaping (Galatians 6:7). If an adult's positive influence had been stronger than the pull of the crowd when the seed was being planted, he might never have reached for the first bottle.

"It's better to establish values early in life that will carry them over the critical years," Lew says.

Life is not summer camp, and we are not counselors. A child with one less buddy and one more adult willing to help establish appropriate values by setting limits through discipline may be changed forever.

Chapter Three

TRUST AND GENEROSITY

So that your trust may be in the LORD,
I teach you today, even you.
—Proverbs 22:19

Children who have been lied to by their parents and others they once trusted no longer trust anybody. When they meet you, they will assume you are another liar. Only honesty and time will change them.

Trust often grows out of generosity—not giving children everything they want but giving them what they *need*. "A generous man will himself be blessed" (Proverbs 22:9). If you are generous with your time, the thing children need most, you will be blessed with their trust.

I've read surveys that show how little time parents spend with their children, and I wonder how they expect to build a relationship in just a few minutes a day. Many parents, including folks who work at Chick-fil-A, have a shortage of time with their families. That's one reason why we close all of our restaurants on Sunday, so that families can be guaranteed at least one day a week together.

Knowing that time is tight and that you have only a few years to make the strongest positive impact on your children, don't spend your precious family days on the golf course or watching sports on television all afternoon. Don't consider watching TV with your children to be "quality time." You may be in the same room, but you're not together. Participate in activities with your children. Play games together. Seek opportunities to be with them on their turf. Volunteer to coach their sports team, lead their Scout troop, or teach their Sunday school class.

If you are generous with your time, you will be blessed with the trust of a child.

Then communicate. But don't expect them to share their feelings on your schedule. You have to wait patiently. When our children were young and I came home from work, I'd ask, "How are things?"

They'd say, "Good."

And that was the end of the conversation.

I learned that when you talk to children, a conversation won't happen when it's convenient for you but when it's convenient for them. You never call a child in and then say, "Well, let's talk." The child won't have anything to say. But if you're around children long enough, they'll open up and start to share their problems or opportunities. When they do, you'd better stop whatever you're doing to listen because the opportunity may not come around again for a while.

One weekend when our daughter, Trudy, was home from college, she told me, "Dad, the thing I remember most about you are the times you sat at my bedside and let me tell you all the things I did that day." All the possessions we had shared with her—clothes, a car, a nice house to grow up in—were secondary to those times we spent together at bedtime talking.

Small Moments, Big Changes

When we share our time with children, the little things often become lifetime memories for them. My friend Jeff Manley recently reminded me of an incident I long ago forgot. Jeff's father was an alcoholic, and when Jeff was a teenager, his father took his own life. I saw Jeff at camp a little while later out on the front porch of one of the cabins. I hugged him, then we sat in the rocking chairs for a while talking. "We probably didn't talk for more than ten minutes," Jeff recalls, "but when I got home from camp, you called to see how I was doing."

When we share our time with children, the little things often become lifetime memories for them.

Jeff has carried the memory of those two little things, an arm around the shoulder and a telephone call, for years now. The call led to a deeper friendship. I don't remember all the topics Jeff and I talked about, but he remembers our business discussions. "I had never had a man talk to me about his day at the office," he recalls, "sharing with me what he cared about and asking me for my opinion. It really was neat."

The thing is, I liked Jeff and truly valued his opinion. Today Jeff manages The Rock Ranch, where we have two foster homes.

Be Generous with Encouragement

How do you know when a child needs encouragement?

If he or she is breathing.

One of the saddest letters I ever received came from the mother of a boy I had become friends with. Mike was a teenager with lots of potential, and I reminded him of that often. We talked about where he might go to college and what his career choices might be. After a while, though, I received a letter from Mike's mother telling me I was giving Mike false hopes. "Mike can't live up to what you encourage him to be and what you expect him to do," she wrote.

Mike was getting no encouragement at home, the one place where he should get it most.

If I continued, she said, I would make Mike feel guilty for his failure. Mike was getting no encouragement at home, the one place where he should get it most. If his mother had offered genuine encouragement and recognized his accomplishments, they could have experienced together the joy that comes with hope.

Jeff Manley overheard me tell someone on the telephone, "You need to meet Jeff. He's a fine boy—a big

How do you know if a child

needs encouragement?

If he or she is breathing.

boy and a hard worker." Jeff says it was the first time he had ever received a compliment from a man, and he suddenly believed he had a good reputation to live up to.

Accountability can reinforce encouragement. One week in Sunday school I was encouraging the boys not to smoke cigarettes. After class, Wayne told me that even though both of his parents smoked, he had never smoked a cigarette. When I asked him how he was able to avoid the temptation, he said that he and his sister, who was two years older, had vowed to each other that they would never smoke. Through the years they held each other accountable to that vow. I have often encouraged Wayne and praised him for his decision. He came to work with us at Chick-fil-A as a teenager, and now he has been operating a Chick-fil-A restaurant for many years, encouraging the young people who work there to make good decisions and holding them accountable.

Appropriate rewards can also reinforce encouragement. When Richard came to live in one of our foster homes, he became the first person in his family to graduate from high school. I gave him a watch with his name and graduation date engraved on the back, and I told him I would give him a ring when he graduated from college. Richard completed college because he knew people cared about him, loved him, and wanted him to succeed, and today he wears his ring as the reward for his accomplishment through hard work.

Be Generous with Hospitality

Make your home a place where children want to visit.

Years ago Jeannette and I hosted barn parties and hayrides for kids. We even had a greasy pig chase. And I often invited my Sunday school boys out to our farm to ride horses or motorbikes. They rode all over the place—across pastures, through the woods, and down by the river. Jeannette and I tried to create an atmosphere where they could relax and have fun. In those comfortable surroundings I was also able to let them know what I expected of them: to make good decisions and to stay out of trouble. Those afternoons were like an extension of Sunday school; they saw us attempting to put into action the Bible lessons I had taught them.

Throughout the years some of the boys have come out to the farm during the week because they know it is a quiet, safe place. With 262 acres, they can walk for a long time without even coming up to the house. One of the boys has told me he would ride his bike from home—fourteen miles—just to come walk down by the river and pray.

Our children have carried on the tradition of hospitality by opening their homes to large groups of young people, who enjoy a wholesome environment free of alcohol and open marital disputes.

Hospitality may be one of the most effective ways of touching young lives. Our son Bubba, who enjoys clowning around with the kids who visit, also says, "I don't mind checking the kids out spiritually. At times that makes our own children uncomfortable, but they realize that's the way I am."

The man thought he had been singled out, and he remembered that at least one person cared enough to hug him.

Be Generous with Affection

My good friend Charlie "Tremendous" Jones greets people in an unusual way. He gives every man he meets a big hug. "Everybody needs a hug," he says.

A sincere handshake, a hug, a kiss on the cheek—all these signs of affection remind others that we care about them. Charlie tells of a man who wrote him from prison, introducing himself by saying, "I'm the person you hugged." The man thought he had been singled out, and he remembered that at least one person cared enough to hug him.

I met a little boy at the children's home we founded in Brazil, and every time I saw him I said, "I love you, Michael." Michael did not speak English, and I did not speak Portuguese, but I kept repeating those words: "I love you, Michael." We played together, and several nights I rocked him to sleep. When the time came for Jeannette and me to go home, Michael wrapped his little arms around my leg and didn't want to let me leave. He and I both cried, and we understood how much we loved each other. And it all began with a simple hug.

I hope that whenever I give a gift to a child, that child knows the gift does not come from me but from God, the source of all good gifts.

BE GENEROUS WITH THE GLORY

We all want to get credit for the things we do. But if we want to instill humility, generosity, and other important character traits in children, we must model those traits ourselves. Many times that means stepping out of the limelight and letting others receive praise. Robert W. Woodruff, president of The Coca-Cola

Company for more than sixty years, displayed promi-
nently on his desk his personal creed: "There is no limit
to what a man can do or where he can go if he doesn't
mind who gets the credit."

I hope that whenever I give a gift to a child, that
child knows the gift does not come from me but from
God, the source of all good gifts. With that understand-
ing, the gift takes on greater significance for both of us.

When Children Learn Generosity

Trudy, her husband, John, and their children came
back for their first furlough from Brazil, where they were
serving as missionaries. Within a few days their son John
was longing to see one of his buddies. He asked Trudy if
he could send a present back to Ednei, and Trudy explained that it would have to be something small because of the shipping expense. John had already decided
what to send—a package of rubber bands.

"Whenever we play," he explained, "Ednei likes to
dig rubber bands out of the trash can and flip them off
the wall."

So John mailed the rubber bands to Ednei, and when
the family returned to Brazil, Ednei was still beaming.
Those rubber bands were the first brand new thing he

had ever owned in his life. His clothes, his shoes, and his toys had all been hand-me-downs.

That little package of rubber bands had a lasting impact on Ednei, because through them he had experienced the generosity and love of a true friend. They also had a tremendous impact on John, who saw the effect of his generosity on someone else.

When Children Learn Trust

My friend Hal King's father, a popular high school band director, was murdered when Hal was thirteen years old. Hal's grandfather, who was mayor of Brunswick, Georgia, might have stepped in to spend more time with his grandchildren, but Hal recalls, "My grandfather was a very busy man, and he lived too far away from Atlanta."

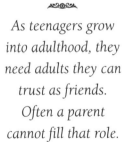

As teenagers grow into adulthood, they need adults they can trust as friends. Often a parent cannot fill that role.

Hal says I was the first older man to treat him like a friend. Hal *was* my friend, and that's an important distinction. If you simply act like a friend to children, they will see through you in a minute. Your actions must be motivated by a sincere desire to be a friend. If you don't have that desire, pray for it.

As teenagers grow into adulthood, they need adults they can trust as friends. Often a parent cannot fill that role. But as Hal's Sunday school teacher, I had an opportunity to earn his trust and become his friend. And as his friend, I could talk with Hal about things his father might have told him if he had lived.

Hal went with me to the opening of a new Chick-fil-A restaurant in North Carolina, and that night we prayed together. He says he was uncomfortable—nobody had ever shown him how to pray on his knees—but it became his habit. He learned through prayer that there is not a single person—not a parent or even a best friend—that he can trust as much as his heavenly Father. And no person will be as generous.

"What greater gift can a father have than to see his daughter going to our Father in trust?"

As a husband and a father, Hal has led his family into that kind of trusting relationship. "One night I knocked on my seventeen-year-old daughter's door," he says, "and she didn't answer. The light was off, and I thought she was asleep, so I was just going to peep in. But when the light spilled in, I saw her on her knees with her head on the floor, where she had been weeping and praying. I started to cry in thankfulness to God. What greater gift can a father have than to see his daughter going to our Father in trust?"

Chapter Four

COMMON SENSE

A prudent man sees danger and takes refuge,
but the simple keep going and suffer for it.
        —*Proverbs 22:3*

Common sense is not as common as people think. Children are not born with common sense. They have to learn it by making mistakes or by witnessing the mistakes of others. It's difficult for an adult to teach common sense to a child; you may be more effective by creating opportunities or responding to opportunities that allow the child to develop common sense.

Here are a few ways parents multiply a child's *lack* of common sense:

- Give him a big weekly allowance.

- Give her a brand new car when she turns sixteen.
- Protect him from the consequences of his bad decisions.

SOWING AND REAPING

Helping boys and girls develop common sense requires a relationship, and it requires trust. I enjoy teaching Sunday school to thirteen-year-old boys because I can spend an entire year building relationships with them. We often talk about morals as well as common sense as they grow into the age where they will make decisions—good or bad—that will have lasting consequences. At age thirteen boys are quickly becoming men. They're physically able to handle a horse and a small motorbike, and they're mature enough to take more responsibility. In fact, in recent years I have considered dropping back and teaching eleven-year-old boys, because these days by the time they're thirteen, some children have already set their lives on a course for trouble, and they can be hard to reach. It's an important time to reinforce the lessons they have learned before they step into adulthood.

I first knew Kevin when he was thirteen years old and he came to my Sunday school class. We've kept in touch, and when he visited me a few weeks before his most recent trouble, he looked much older than his years. He's made many poor choices, and now he's reaping a multitude of troubles. You are aware of the principle of sowing and reaping: "Whatsoever a man soweth, that shall he also reap" (Galatians 6:7, KJV). I've found that you reap much more than you sow, just as a kernel of corn planted yields much more than a single kernel. Sow a seed of trouble, and you'll harvest a bushel of sorrow.

> *I've found that you reap much more than you sow, just as a kernel of corn planted yields much more than a single kernel. Sow a seed of trouble, and you'll harvest a bushel of sorrow.*

Kevin, for example, is not violent; he's just not responsible. And his irresponsibility and poor choices have made a disaster of his life.

"I used to hate responsibility," he says. "I despised it. I wanted to be responsible for me and nobody else."

Kevin also lacked patience. Instead of going to college, he got a job building houses. And when he didn't earn as much money as he wanted doing that, he started selling drugs to make some fast cash. Then he got caught.

I'm convinced that Kevin wants to do the right thing. He's married and has a child, and he wants to do right by his family. But he continues to sow bad seed. He was riding his motorcycle a few weeks after our lunch when a policeman stopped him for a traffic violation. Kevin didn't have a driver's license—his had been revoked—and he was still on parole after his most recent time in prison. Now his parole has been revoked and he's back in prison.

Prodigals in Our Time

One of the most retold stories in the Bible is the parable of the prodigal son, about a young man who lacks common sense. The young man asks his father for his inheritance in advance, and the father, rather than question his son's sensibility, gives him everything he desires. The prodigal then does what many young men with easy money would do: he squanders his wealth in wild living and winds up penniless.

Like the prodigal, my friend Eric came into a lot of money long before he was able to handle the consequences of it. Eric was a teenager living in Florida when he found some jewelry alongside a railroad track. An honest boy, he did the right thing and turned the jewels over to the police. After six months and several

Things I Wish I Had Known Before I Was Twenty-One

That my health after thirty depended in a large degree on what I put into my stomach before I was twenty-one.

How to take care of money.

That a man's habits are mighty hard to change after he is twenty-one.

That a harvest depends upon the seeds sown.

The worthwhile things require time, patience, and work.

That you cannot get something for nothing.

The folly of not taking older people's advice.

The value of absolute truthfulness in everything.

That what Mother wanted me to do was right.

Dad wasn't an old fogy after all.

More of the helpful and inspiring messages of the Bible.

The greatness of the opportunity and joy of serving a fellow human being.

That Jesus Christ wants to be my Savior and Friend.

newspaper articles, no one had claimed the prize, so the police gave the jewels back to Eric. They were valued at more than $1 million.

Eric was living with his aunt, and she hired a lawyer to help manage the money, but as soon as Eric turned eighteen, he had complete legal control of his wealth. The lawyer, who was a friend of mine, told me about his client, and I said I would like to meet Eric.

I invited Eric to the opening of a new Chick-fil-A restaurant in his town, and afterward he came to our condominium nearby. As soon as he stepped inside, he lit a cigarette. I learned that evening that Eric was a high school dropout, that he had worked odd jobs around the neighborhood, and that much of his new-found money was going for drugs. He already was beginning to realize the truth of his new situation. "I wish I hadn't found that jewelry," he told me. "Whenever I go out with friends, they expect me to pick up the tab for drinks and food." In other words, he was realizing the value his friends placed in him.

Later, Eric's aunt said the money was "the worst thing that could have happened to him. I had him outside weed-eating grass one day, and the next-door neighbor called over, 'Why is a millionaire doing a job like that?'"

She had a hard time getting him to do any work after that.

Eric's brother called me recently and arranged a meeting for us. It's been nearly twenty years since Eric became a millionaire, and now he is broke. He's lost every tooth in his mouth, and at age thirty-six, he looks sixty-six. He's mentally unable to care for himself and, unlike the biblical prodigal, he has no earthly father to go home to. Eric's brother and aunt are doing what they can for him.

Eric became a millionaire, and now he is broke. He's lost every tooth in his mouth, and at age thirty-six, he looks sixty-six.

GROWING IN COMMON SENSE

In time and with training, both Eric and the prodigal son might have matured enough to handle the wealth they received. Unfortunately, parents too seldom spend the time to teach their children important life skills.

In our foster homes we begin to teach responsibility with money as early as possible. Houseparents, for example, clip coupons from the newspaper before they go to the grocery store. It takes a little extra time, but it's a good way to show the children how much money they can save if they're prudent.

All of the children have savings accounts, and I encourage them to add to it by matching their savings dollar for dollar. As in all things, some children are better than others at saving. Some learn, for example, that they can save more money if they drink tap water instead of soft drinks.

The Wages of the Prodigal

Recently I met a teenage boy with an outgoing personality who said he hoped to work for Chick-fil-A someday. We lined him up with one of our restaurant Operators and put him to work right away.

The boy worked hard and soon earned a position as crew leader. Then one afternoon he called me in tears. He said he had made a terrible mistake and asked if he could come talk with me.

He explained that one Saturday night when closing the restaurant, the Operator had let him take home some leftover Chick-fil-A Cool Wraps™. But rather than share them with his family, he took them to school the following Monday and sold them, despite our rules prohibiting him from doing that. He did it a couple more times and realized he had found a way to earn some extra money.

Then he decided to sell a few more on other days of

the week, so at the end of his shift at the restaurant, he would slip out with a few Cool Wraps.

An administrator at the school called the Operator and told him what was happening. My young friend, when confronted with the facts, admitted the theft, and the Operator fired him. The boy came to my home and asked me to forgive him. I did, and he remains my friend. But because his behavior was a pattern of deception

My friend sacrificed his good name and reputation for a few dollars.

and theft, not just a single incident, I didn't see how we could allow him back behind the counter.

My friend had sacrificed his good name and reputation for a few dollars and learned a difficult lesson about being a good steward of things entrusted to him.

PRODIGALS WITH THEIR OWN CAR KEYS

Steve was doing some work for me, and one day he drove up in his car with a tag that read, "Born to Raise Hell!"

"What do you mean, putting a tag like that on your car?" I asked him.

He said, "My daddy gave it to me."

I knew then that Steve's father was lacking in common sense, and he was passing his deficiency on to his son—along with the keys to a car.

One of the quickest ways to turn sixteen-year-old children into prodigals is to give them their own car. They don't have the common sense to take on that much responsibility at age sixteen, and statistics on accidents and deaths on the highway bear me out.

My friend Mike turned sixteen and his father gave him a new car. Mike's parents were divorced, and he was living with his mother. Giving Mike a car, the father believed, would allow Mike to come visit him without the father having to go pick him up every weekend.

A few months later Mike's dad told me, "Since I gave him that car, he doesn't have time to see me anymore. He's off with his friends doing other things."

The father wanted to take away the car at that point, but it was too late. That would have been like taking cotton candy from a three-year-old, and he didn't have the strength to do it.

Our three children had to wait until they were eighteen before they got their own cars, although my car was available to them whenever they needed it. At age sixteen children will act differently in their father's car than they will in their own. When they received their own cars, I tried to impress upon each of them that it was still their Father's car.

Our oldest child, Dan, picked out a Pontiac Firebird. It was delivered on his eighteenth birthday, and I added a surprise. On the dashboard I had a nameplate installed that read, "Custom made for Dan Cathy. Matthew 6:33."

At age sixteen children will act differently in their father's car than they will in their own.

Dan looked up Matthew 6:33 and read, "Seek ye first the kingdom of God, and his righteousness; and all these things shall be added unto you" (KJV).

My message to Dan through that nameplate, which he read every day for years, was that the gift was not from his earthly father but from his heavenly Father, and he should accept and respect it as a gift from God. Bubba and Trudy also received a new automobile when they turned eighteen, and they each had a verse of scripture inside. Now my grandchildren, as they turn eighteen, are receiving a car with a Bible verse on the dashboard, and I rest easier when they're out, knowing they will be more responsible with a gift that came from God.

That important distinction—that all of our good gifts are from God—allows us to be much more generous in sharing those gifts with others. And those receiving the gifts are more likely to apply their common sense when using them.

Common Sense and Everyday Living

One of the most important classes I took in high school was called Everyday Living. Among the many things I learned was how to manage and balance a checkbook, how to dress for an interview, and common courtesies.

When children are four or five years old, they can shake hands firmly and look another person in the eye.

Adults should begin teaching children basic living skills early in life. When they're four or five years old, they can learn to separate their clothes into colors and whites. They can sweep the floor and clean the bathroom. They can shake hands firmly and look another person in the eye.

Children who have not been taught basic living skills at home will act years younger than their peers. Don't blame children for things they have not been taught. Teach them. Every Eagle Scout begins as a Tenderfoot. But if nobody takes the time to teach him how to tie a square knot, he will never advance.

A boy who sits with me in church is a recent high school graduate. When he was in my Sunday school class several years ago, he was always the last boy to come in and the first to leave. He didn't seem to be close to the other boys in class. His father had died after being gone from the home for several years. When my friend moved up to the next grade, he stopped going to Sunday school, so I invited him back to my class for another year or two. His mother and my wife both sing in the choir, so he sits with me every Sunday. A child can learn many basic living skills by simply spending time with adults if we will make ourselves available.

Common Sense and Personal Appearance

Despite what people say about beauty being only skin-deep, the first impression we make on people is with our outward appearance. After my picture appeared on the cover of a national magazine, I received a letter from a woman who told me, "I'm not photogenic either."

We can't do much about the face God gave us, but we can take care of some things like grooming, hygiene, and the clothes we wear.

My friend Terry had been working in the stock room of a company in Atlanta, and he hoped to be promoted someday. But he dressed poorly every day, and his hair was down his back. "They don't care how I look down where I work," he said. "I'll get it cut when I get promoted."

But I told him he wasn't going to get promoted until he started looking like someone his employer might want to move out of the stock room.

"Mr. Cathy," he said, "it's not the way you look on the outside that matters. What really matters is who you are on the inside."

"That's absolutely right," I replied. "What's on the inside matters most. But I can't see your insides. All I can see is what's on the outside—the things you do and say, the way you dress, and your haircut. They say things about you."

Then I asked him if he took into account a girl's appearance before he asked her for a date. He admitted that he did, even though a girl who didn't take care of her looks might make a better wife and a wonderful mother for his children. He finally woke up to the fact that personal appearance is important.

Teach Common Sense Gently

Many teenagers who appear to lack common sense are merely avoiding any interaction with adults. They have been abused or lied to so many times, they decide to take care of themselves or turn to other children for help.

A child had been living in one of our foster homes for more than a year when the family was planning a vacation. The boy didn't have a suitcase, but he knew there were several suitcases in the closet. However, instead of asking his house-parents if he could use one of those suitcases, he offered one of the other children five dollars to use his.

On the face of it, the boy appeared to be lacking common sense. But this child was simply doing everything he could to avoid standing out from the crowd.

On the face of it, the boy appeared to be lacking common sense. But this child was simply doing everything he could to avoid standing out from the crowd.

You may never know the motivation behind the

actions of some children who appear to lack common sense. Be patient with them, and don't assume they are stupid. They may simply be protecting themselves the best way they know how.

Chapter Five

RIGHT CROWD, WRONG CROWD

Do not make friends with a hot-tempered man,
do not associate with one easily angered,
or you may learn his ways and get yourself ensnared.
—Proverbs 22:24-25

I recently read a survey indicating peer pressure had surpassed parents as the strongest influence in the lives of American teenagers. We must do everything in our power, then, to positively influence the influencers.

RECRUIT POSITIVE ROLE MODELS

Teenagers and preteens idolize and imitate college

students. Houseparents Doug and Julie Bowling take advantage of that fact by actively seeking college students with high moral standards and strong character, then creating opportunities for their children to spend time with them.

> *Doug and Julie actively seek college students with high moral standards and strong character, then create opportunities for their children to spend time with them.*

Recently Julie has been mentoring a Berry College sophomore who plays on the women's basketball team and is a great Christian girl. She comes by the house to visit Julie, then spends time with the children, who hang all over her.

The Bowlings also host a Bible study in their home led by a Berry student who brings his guitar and teaches the children chords before the students arrive. As many as seventy-five college students have attended, and the Bowlings' kids participate in the first part of the program.

Intentionally seek influencers for the children you want to influence, then create opportunities for them to be together. Take them to a ballgame or hire them to babysit. Then watch what happens.

Two-Word Attitude Adjustment

Chick-fil-A restaurant Operators adhere to the same principle when hiring team members. They know it's much easier to hire a good attitude than to change a bad one. They also know that every smile they hire is infectious. But every attitude can take a little adjustment.

Good habits can bridge the gap on those days when we aren't feeling super. For example, a few years ago I asked everyone at Chick-fil-A to say "My pleasure" whenever anyone thanked them. Almost immediately I began receiving letters from customers commenting on our courteous people.

Saying "My pleasure" instead of "You're welcome" or "No problem" also reminded each of us that we truly do enjoy our work and serving others, even on our bad days. Like most good habits, it's a little thing that makes a big difference.

Bad Attitudes Are Infectious Too

I asked my friend Kevin what he thought it might take to keep him out of trouble. This was at our lunch a few weeks before his most recent incarceration. He sat across the table from me and said, "I'm at the point in my life now where I have to put 100 percent effort into keeping out of trouble and doing the right thing. If I don't, I'll be in jail."

He said his wife helps by trying to keep him away from his old friends who are still doing bad things. "But I can't walk away from the guys I've known all my life," he confessed.

When he tells her he's going to hang out with the guys, she immediately says, "I'll come with you." She knows the power of negative influence. Proverbs 22:25 warns that when you hang around with the wrong crowd, you may learn their ways and get yourself ensnared. Kevin can't blame all his troubles on his friends, but if he had followed his wife's good advice, he might be home with his family instead of in prison.

The Power of Sex

I am no longer amazed by the stories I hear from children. Brokenhearted, but not amazed.

Shortly after a boy came to live in one of our foster homes, he and I were talking about his mother. I asked him what kind of work she did.

"She takes off her clothes and dances," he said. "Everything but her shoes."

I was stunned that this little boy would know such

a thing about his mother, and I hoped he was mistaken. I asked, "How do you know that?"

"Sometimes I have to go with her to work," he said.

How is that child going to make responsible moral decisions when he grows up? His mother, more than anybody, should understand the power of sex to destroy a life.

Proverbs 22:14 says, "The mouth of an adulteress is a deep pit; he who is under the LORD's wrath will fall into it."

In the time since I began working on this book, two of the young men I admire most—men I have known and loved since they were young teens—have fallen into adulterous relationships, and it breaks my heart.

William (not his real name) was in my Sunday school class as a boy, and through the years he had impressed me so much with his generosity, I asked him to talk to my Sunday school class one morning. But when Sunday came around, he didn't show up. He came to church after class and told me that he couldn't face the boys that morning because of some family problems he was having. I asked if it was anything I could help him with, and he said another woman had come into his life through his work. They had gone to lunch together and had shared each other's problems. He was attracted to her. He was being tempted.

William asked me to pray that God might help him overcome the temptation he was experiencing, and we prayed together.

On Tuesday morning William's wife called and told me William had not come home the night before. I later learned that William had spent the previous Friday night—before we met at church—with the woman from work.

Not long after that William left his wife and their two small children and moved into an apartment with his girlfriend, who is married and has an eight-year-old daughter.

I called William and tried to reason with him—to convince him that he was making a terrible mistake. But he said, "She loves me and I love her."

"You don't love her," I said. "You love each other's bodies, but you don't love each other. Wait until you get sick or something like that and have to have someone to nurse you, and then see how far your love goes. And what about your wife?"

"I love her too," he said.

"Do you?" I asked. "What's the seventh commandment?"

"Thou shalt not commit adultery," he said. He had learned the answer a dozen years earlier in my Sunday school class.

"What's the seventh commandment?" I asked again.

"Thou shalt not commit adultery," he said.

"What's the seventh commandment?" I asked once more.

"Thou shalt not commit adultery," he said, almost in tears. God gives us the gift of a conscience—a way of telling us when we're going in the wrong direction—and William's conscience was working on him.

God gives us the gift of a conscience—a way of telling us when we're going in the wrong direction.

"Tell me again, William," I said hoping my words and his conscience would shake him up. I tried to drive the point home for him. He knows what he's doing, but he says he's willing to accept the consequences.

William will suffer the consequences of his decision—for ignoring his conscience and doing what he knew was wrong. And the pain will be felt by his children, just as William felt similar pain years ago. You see, William grew up in a divided home. His father had a problem with alcohol and left his family for another woman. William had told me years ago of his bitter experiences as a child in that situation. Now he's putting his children through the same thing.

ONE TIME WILL HURT

Young people are naturally curious about drugs, alcohol, and sex. They want to experiment, and they tell themselves, "One time won't hurt." So they try it just once, and nothing bad happens. They don't get caught. The girl didn't get pregnant. So they do it again. And again. And before long they have a habit, and they begin to reap the consequences of their initial decision.

A boy who had been in my Sunday school class was having problems in his home. He was fifteen years old, and he called to tell me he had gotten the neighbor girl pregnant.

"I didn't mean to do that," he said, and he went on to describe the circumstances. He didn't want to tell his parents what had happened, and he wanted my help.

"There's no way I can help you," I said. "You're just going to have to face up to your parents, and they're going to have to help you."

REMAINING PURE

The word *sex* was never spoken in my home when I was a child. My mother, my dad, and my Sunday school teacher never mentioned sex. Sex was not taught in school when I was coming along. The only place I found out about sex was in the school yard, and I didn't understand a lot about it, like how some girls got pregnant and others didn't. I had no one to ask.

Adults still feel uncomfortable talking to children about sex. And the world is telling kids so much about it that if you wait too long, they'll know more than you do. They're getting too much sex "education" from television, magazines, and the Internet.

Adults still feel uncomfortable talking to children about sex. And the world is telling kids so much about it that if you wait too long, they'll know more than you do.

If our children are to remain pure, we must do three things:

- Pray for them
- Model purity
- Talk to them about remaining pure

This is your responsibility as a parent. It's your job.

When I talk with young people about sex, I tell them how important it is to present their bodies to their spouse unstained—to remain a virgin until marriage. What a gift you can give your mate!

If you choose otherwise, I tell them, it reminds me of the merchandise you find in the bargain basement of the department store. There's a sign that says "slightly stained," and the price is greatly reduced.

It reminds me of the merchandise you find in the bargain basement of the department store. There's a sign that says "slightly stained," and the price is greatly reduced.

It takes a tremendous amount of self-control, especially in this world, to remain pure. The key is to avoid putting yourself into a position where temptations and opportunities arise.

I've often told my Sunday school boys that sex is God's gift to individuals, but it's the devil's playground. So a lot of boys get in trouble just playing around—putting their hands where they shouldn't be, stimulating themselves to the point of no return.

It happens so many times—a girl comes in and tells her mother she's pregnant, and she didn't even plan to have sex. But if the situation is right and the temptation is great, wrong things can happen.

Some churches encourage their young people to sign a commitment that they will abstain from sex until they're married. If a child decides in advance that the answer is "no," then he or she may find it easier to say no to compromising situations.

Our children have asked our grandchildren to make a commitment to remaining pure. For example, Trudy and John present each of their children a promise ring on their fifteenth birthday, and the child receiving the ring signs a commitment:

> With this ring, I promise, before God, my parents, my sisters, and my brother . . . that my body will remain pure and holy. I agree to restrain from any sexual conduct that would contradict Christian principles taught to me by my parents based on God's Holy Word. This ring will be a constant reminder to me of God's great love and faithfulness to live His life through me. Whenever tempted to give into my sexual desires, this ring will help me recall Psalm 46:1: "God is my refuge and strength, a

very present help in trouble."

Upon receiving this ring, I also promise to abstain from any use of alcohol, drugs, or tobacco. With this commitment, I can present to my future wife a vessel clean and beautiful. In turn, I ask the Lord to give to me a wife whose past has been equally committed to my Lord—never having yielded to premarital sex, alcohol, drugs, or tobacco. I am committed to search and wait for such a woman, so that our lives together can begin within God's plan for marriage.

Trudy, John, and all the children also sign the commitment as witnesses, and in doing so they each are reminded of the commitment to purity they made, or will make when they turn fifteen.

Notice the emphasis on abstinence from alcohol and drug use. I remind teenagers that one of the quickest ways to find themselves in compromising situations is through alcohol.

I learned from my children the power of modeling abstinence. Years ago when I was actively involved in the Georgia Restaurant Association, I attended events

One of the quickest ways to find yourself in a compromising situation is through alcohol.

where wine was served, and occasionally I would have a glass. Then when our children came along, Jeannette and I decided never to have wine at our table. Our children were watching us closely, and we didn't want to send the wrong message about what we said and did.

Another time our family was at a dinner where there was a wine tasting. I was curious about the various wines, and I picked up a glass. Trudy asked, "Daddy, you aren't going to drink that, are you?"

I put it down quickly and said, "No, I'm not."

She was putting me to the test. Children are always putting us to the test, whether we know it or not. We must be aware of the messages we send.

Inspirational speaker Zig Ziglar tells a similar story about his son. Zig had stopped drinking after asking himself the question, "Does it glorify God?" Not long after that, he and his wife went out to celebrate their anniversary. The owner of the restaurant, who was a friend of theirs, gave them a bottle of wine, "But I didn't have the courage at that point to say, 'We don't drink,'" Zig recalls, and they drank some of the wine.

When they got home, their seven-year-old son asked, "Dad, did you drink any wine or anything?"

Zig admitted that they had, and he recalls, "If I live

to be 1,000, I'll never forget his exact words. He looked right at me and softly said, 'Dad, I can't begin to tell you how disappointed I am in you.'"

Children are watching everything we do.

The world is also testing us. Our family was on vacation at Daytona Beach, and I suggested that we go watch the dogs run at the racetrack. Again Trudy, who was an adult by then, spoke up and asked, "Dad, are we really going in there? Is that a place where you would take your Sunday school boys?"

I explained that we weren't going to do any gambling or drinking. We were just going to watch the dogs run.

So we went in, and we didn't stay long. As we left I heard someone holler, "Hey, Truett Cathy!" as though he was announcing to the world that I had arrived. Of course, I assumed he was there to gamble, and I'm sure he assumed the same of me. We must be careful about what we say and do, not only to keep ourselves pure, but because people, especially children, are watching us and taking their cues from us.

As our culture continues to bombard young people with sexual images and temptations, I try to think of other ways to reverse the trend. I've even considered offering a monetary reward for remaining sexually pure, but Jeannette reminds me that we shouldn't pay people for doing something that's right.

You may wonder why, in this day when "everybody's doing it," I speak out so strongly against premarital sex. I believe God requires abstinence because He knows that sex is a potential time bomb in our marriage. A person who has had premarital sex is more likely to engage in adultery—and risk family devastation. William has told me that was the case with him. His wife was two months pregnant when they married. "At least he did the honorable thing and married her," some will say. And sometimes marriages that begin after pregnancy work out remarkably well.

But we must do more than talk. We must model the good behavior.

Unfortunately for William's family, and thousands of others, one form of sexual misconduct begets another.

So I will continue to talk about abstinence with my Sunday school students. Preachers will preach on the subject, and youth directors will talk with their young people about it. But we must do more than talk. We must model the good behavior. We must become the "right crowd"—the kind of people we want children to spend time with and be influenced by.

Chapter Six

STABILITY

Drive out the mocker, and out goes strife;
quarrels and insults are ended.

—Proverbs 22:10

T he greatest gift you can give children is a stable home to grow up in. Children who do not have stability at home seek stable relationships with other adults. Live up to your marriage commitment, and children are more likely to trust you and believe that you will not shirk your commitment to them.

A Family Built on Instability

Michael O'Kelley and his six brothers were in turmoil when I met them. Michael was only ten years old. His eighteen-year-old brother Terry was the family patriarch. Three years earlier, when their mother lay on her deathbed, Terry had promised her that he would keep the boys together after she was gone. They all moved in with their grandfather until he died. Their father, who had abandoned them earlier, returned long enough to sell whatever assets he could find and empty the bank accounts. He later pleaded guilty to child abandonment and theft charges.

The boys were left without enough money to bury their grandfather or pay their mother's medical bills, so Terry and sixteen-year-old Tommy dropped out of high school to get jobs and keep the boys together.

The local media began to tell the story of the brothers' commitment to one another, and the community reached out to them with donations. I read about the O'Kelley brothers in the newspaper, and I wanted to help. I thought the younger boys might do well in our foster home, but because of the vow Terry had made to his mother, he didn't want them to move.

I contacted the O'Kelleys and got to know them, then I helped get them into the egg business with three chicken houses and a three-bedroom farmhouse. I even moved in with them for several days to help them get started, and every morning the seven boys and I went out to gather eggs. They all worked hard, even eight-year-old Jason.

The O'Kelley brothers were totally committed to one another. But you can't ask an eighteen-year-old boy to assume financial and parental responsibilities for his six younger brothers. Terry knew almost nothing about being a father, and the boys ran wild. I bought some bunk beds for them, and when I went back to visit a few weeks later, they were broken.

The O'Kelley brothers were totally committed to one another. But you can't ask an eighteen-year-old boy to assume financial and parental responsibilities for his six younger brothers.

"We were rough on furniture," Michael says, looking back.

With the help of a Chick-fil-A Operator, we got a Chevrolet Suburban for the boys so they could all fit in one vehicle. By Thanksgiving of that year they had traded the Suburban for a Camaro and a pickup truck. They were more interested in meeting their personal desires than their needs. They were typical boys with no adult to rein them in.

All the time, however, they continued to work hard

in the egg business. Otherwise they would not have survived.

When a fire in one of their henhouses put the boys out of business, Terry and Tommy found jobs, Terry in a poultry processing plant and Tommy as a diesel mechanic. That left the younger boys with even less supervision. To make things worse, their story caught the eye of a movie production company, which bought the rights. Each boy got $28,000. Suddenly they had money in their pockets, but they knew almost nothing about how to manage it, and they weren't interested in taking advice from well-meaning neighbors. They weren't interested in school, and they weren't thinking about the future. They were celebrities.

After nearly three years, Terry O'Kelley realized the enormity of the situation: the younger boys needed stronger adult guidance. Michael and Jason came to live in WinShape Homes with Julie and Doug Bowling.

Jason stayed a few years then went back to live with Terry, who had married but had never finished school. Michael, who was twelve when he arrived at WinShape Homes, stayed until he graduated from high school. He is now married with three children, and he reflects on his years with Julie and Doug. "All of my brothers dropped out of school," he says. "But Doug and Julie stuck with me all the way through. I was never a rocket scientist, but they convinced me that if I graduated, I could accomplish something."

One brother out of seven finished high school, and it was the boy who stayed in the stable home with two parents.

When he graduated, Michael spent several months in Brazil working in our WinShape Home there. "I went there because I

One brother out of seven finished high school, and it was the boy who stayed in the stable home with two parents.

wanted to help other children, and I felt God was calling me in that direction," he says. "It turned out to be the most beautiful place I had ever seen. And so quiet. I had time to reflect on where I had come from and consider where I was going."

Today Michael and his wife, Sarah, believe God is calling them to work with children. "We are still praying about it," he says. "It's a matter of time before we figure out the direction He wants for us.

"You can run from what you have inside—what you've been taught and what you know," he says, "but eventually you'll come back to the morals you were exposed to. The difference is in the way you're raised."

He told Doug and Julie that he is trying to do for his children what they did for him. He and Sarah are providing a stable environment for their family, breaking the generational cycle of instability.

I believe if Doug and Julie or another loving married couple could have stepped into the O'Kelley brothers' lives when they were much younger, the story might have ended differently for all of them. Those boys experienced hardships no child should endure. Their difficulties taught them important lessons, but without adults in their lives every day, they never learned the deeper meaning of their experiences.

COMMITTING TO STABILITY

Foster children never get used to changing "parents." Many of them move frequently from home to home, family to family. When a foster child moves into one of our homes, we tell him or her, "This will be your home forever. This is the home you will bring your children back to so they can see where you grew up." The homes don't change, and neither do the houseparents. In fact, the houseparents or I will occasionally become legal guardian for a child to maintain our relationship. We

"This will be your home

forever. This is the home

you will bring your

children back to so they can

see where you

grew up."

believe becoming a foster parent is not just a job; it's a lifetime commitment.

Children whose early lives were fraught with upheaval don't like even minor changes. After fourteen years, we changed the color of a foster home from blue to white. Children who had grown up in the home, then left and married, came home one weekend and became upset by the change in color as well as changes inside the house. "We grew up in the blue house," one of them said. "And where's the mirror that was on this wall?"

They had lived a life of turmoil until two parents made a lifetime commitment to them. Keeping the house the same color and the furniture in the same place represented stability to them. They are learning now that little things will continue to change, but our commitment to them will not.

Stop the Arguing

I give the boys in my Sunday school class a questionnaire every year, and one of the questions I ask is, "If you could change anything in your home, what would it be?" The number one answer year after year: "I would stop the arguing."

Arguing is the prime source of instability in our

homes. We're all guilty to some extent of arguing, and it can have a devastating effect on our children.

Being in the company of anybody who is arguing, whether it's two business people, two waitresses, or whatever they might be, makes me uncomfortable. Children feel even more uncomfortable when the combatants are their parents, who may not even realize the children are observing everything that goes on. After the parents usher their children off to bed, they solve their problem but fail to tell the children, who wake up the next morning with memories of the disagreement.

We're all guilty to some extent of arguing, and it can have a devastating effect on our children.

One of my Sunday school boys told me his seven-year-old sister heard their parents arguing and asked their mother, "When are you and Daddy going to get a divorce?"

If you have a disagreement with your mate, deal with it out of the children's presence. If you do argue in front of your children, model forgiveness for them as well. Tell your wife you forgive her. Tell your husband you love him, so your children can be confident that the episode is over and you're moving on together in love.

Then "drive out the mocker," as Proverb 22:10 insists. Stop the insults and sarcasm, and the strife will soon subside.

One morning after Sunday school another of my boys told me his parents were having problems. They were fighting all the time, and he was afraid they were going to get a divorce.

The following Saturday I took them a pie from one of our restaurants, and when I got there the father was installing a security system in their home. We spent a brief time visiting, and I told them what their son had related to me. I said I would be praying for them, and as I left I thought about how that father was protecting his home and his family from outside intruders, but his worst enemy was already inside. He had not made the family a place of security for his children.

An Endurance Test

The arguing in many marriages begins, I believe, because young people believe the goal of marriage is happiness. Everything looked rosy on that moonlit night in the convertible where they fell in love. Six months after the honeymoon is over and the bills start coming in, they find out marriage is not what it's cracked up to be.

The daughter of a Chick-fil-A Operator was fortunate to learn that lesson early. She insisted that her father hire her boyfriend to work at the restaurant, and the father gave in and hired the boy. After he worked there a couple of days, the girl saw his work habits and the way he talked with coworkers and realized he wasn't the boy for her. Love is blind, and marriage is an eye opener. Get those eyes open before marriage! Your mate can make you or break you in life, and if the wrong decision leads to divorce, you're never the same again.

Children will never believe in the covenant of marriage unless they see you living it with their own eyes.

Sometimes marriage is an endurance test, but marriage is designed to be a commitment sealed by a covenant. You can't just tell your children this. They'll never believe it unless they see it with their own eyes. You have to live out your covenant for them to see every day.

There have been times in our marriage when Jeannette and I have not seen matters eye to eye. We've had to pray and ask God to help us overcome problems that arose. We may have disagreed about how to discipline the children or other issues that arose in our family. But one thing we both know is that we will always be faithful to each other.

We modeled our faithfulness before our children, and now they practice faithfulness with their spouses. I believe our twelve grandchildren, having lived with faithful parents, will be faithful to their spouses as well.

Maintaining Stability in the Midst of Turmoil

In some circumstances, husbands or wives may be called to faithfulness and forgiveness way beyond what they think they can handle. I was riding my motorcycle one afternoon, and I stopped to watch a Little League baseball game. I knew some of the boys playing, and I found a seat beside a woman I knew who had three sons. We talked for a while, and she told me she was about to file for divorce.

"I know he's running around on me," she said.

I asked her to think seriously about what she was doing—to consider the children, who ranged in age from nine to seventeen.

"If he's running around on you and you're going to be separated and eventually divorced," I said, "then he's going to have the same rights as you for visiting the children. Wait until the day comes when he and his girl-friend come by to pick up your three children to spend the weekend with them. How are you going to react to that?"

That's when the sword stabs the hardest, when you see an outsider coming to pick up your children, taking them away to be in her home.

I absolutely condemn what her husband was doing, but I also reminded her that sometimes it's better to put up with what you're dealing with now than to suffer the consequences of divorce.

The effects of instability in the home can be felt for generations.

Chapter Seven

A GOOD NAME

A good name is rather to be chosen than great riches,
and loving favour rather than silver and gold.
— Proverbs 22:1 (KJV)

A grade-school teacher gave me a tool for living that I have carried in my heart ever since. Each week our teacher asked the students to write a Bible verse and bring it to school on Monday morning. Then she chose one of the verses and wrote it on the blackboard, along with the student's name, and it stayed there all week.

One Monday morning I brought to school Proverbs 22:1: "A good name is rather to be chosen than great riches, and loving favour rather than silver and gold."

Our teacher selected my verse that week. Every day I walked in the room and saw the verse up there with my name beside it, and it made me feel good. Ever since that Monday morning, I have carried Proverbs 22:1 in my heart. It reminds me to tell the truth so that people will trust me, and to pay my debts on time. It reminds me to seek friendships and loving relationships more than the wealth of this world.

Children and teenagers seek an identity, a name, larger than themselves to call their own—a family, a peer group, a troop, a team, a company—and they adapt their behavior to fit the group. A high school football player chooses not to drink or smoke or stay out late because he's "in training." He has a responsibility to his teammates and his coach. A Chick-fil-A team member smiles even though she's exhausted at the end of a long day; she's living up to the Operator's and her customers' expectations.

THE PRICE OF A GOOD NAME

Trudy never forgot a childhood incident that taught her the price of a good name. Jeannette had taken Trudy to her piano lesson, and as they left the teacher's home, Trudy picked up a penny sitting on a table. When they were in the car, Jeannette saw the penny and asked Trudy where she had gotten it.

Trudy told her, and Jeannette said, "You need to take that penny back to him. It's not yours."

"But Mom," Trudy said, "it's just a penny. He won't even miss it."

Jeannette explained that stealing was stealing, no matter how small the theft, and made Trudy take the penny back to her music teacher.

Trudy was mortified, but she learned a valuable lesson she would carry in her heart for a lifetime.

Seeking a Complete Change

Brandon was ashamed of his family name. "My dad was a druggie and went to jail," he recalls. "My mom couldn't hold down a job, and she was in trouble, so my grandmother called DFCS." Brandon and his brother went into the Georgia foster care system, living in eight different homes and attending seven schools before Brandon's eighth birthday.

When he was eight years old, he came to our WinShape Homes and lived with Sonny and Deenie Brooks, who gave him more stability than he had ever experienced. By the time he was twelve, he said their love had led him to "a complete change." He wanted his identity to reflect that change, so he went through the legal process of changing his name. He took his new first name from David Dollar, a foster dad who had been an important positive role model for him when he was younger; his middle name from David Dollar's son James, who had looked up to Brandon as a role model himself and reminded him to live a life worth emulating; and his last name from me, as I was to become his legal guardian.

Another young man, Mack, did a good job for us working in the Chick-fil-A warehouse. One day I saw on a document that his name was Matthew, and I wondered if I should have been calling him Matt instead of Mack. The next time I saw him I asked him if he wanted me to call him Matt.

"No," he said. "I was named after my father, but he wasn't the kind of person I wanted to be like. I didn't want to be a chip off the old block. When I was fifteen, I asked him if I could change my name, and he refused. I asked him again when I was sixteen, and he refused again. When I asked him a year later, he took a picture of me and tore it up, then told me never to mention a name change again."

So he asked people to call him Mack, and as soon as he turned eighteen, he had his legal name changed as well.

A Successful Dad

I may never be as clever as my
    neighbor down the street,
I may never be as wealthy as some
    other men I meet.
I may never have the glory that some
    other men have had,
But I've just got to be successful as
    that little fellow's dad.

There are certain dreams I cherish,
    that I'd like to see come true,
There are things I would like to do.
There are things I would like to
    accomplish before my earthly life
    is through.
But the task I've set my heart on is
    to guide a little lad,
To make myself successful as that
    little fellow's dad.

*Oh, I may never come to glory, I may
  never gather gold,
And when my business life is over, I
  may be considered a failure as
  told.
But the task I've set my heart on is
  to guide a little lad,
To make myself successful as that
  little fellow's dad.*

*It's the one job that I dream of,
The task I think of most,
For if I fail that little fellow, I have
  nothing else to boast.
For the wealth and fame I'd gather,
  all my fortune would be sad,
If I fail to be successful as that little
  fellow's dad.*

       —Author unknown

In another situation, the mother of a boy living in our WinShape Homes wanted her child to come home with her. The woman had several boyfriends, and I asked Department of Family and Children's Services panel reviewing the case whether it mattered that the mother lives first with one man and then another.

"Mr. Cathy," the chairman answered, "it matters to you and it matters to me, but according to the law we can't discriminate. As long as the parents furnish a roof over their head and food on the table and clothes on their backs, we can't separate the child from his mother simply because she has men friends."

So the boy went with his mother. However, when he married several years later, he took his wife's last name and abandoned his own, explaining that he wanted a *good* name.

A Good Name to Live Up To

Some people are just waiting for the challenge of a positive association that they can live up to. In 1972 I invited one of my former Sunday school boys, Wayne Farr, to operate a Chick-fil-A restaurant. Wayne was twenty-three years old and looked nineteen, and some of the older Operators called him "High School Harry."

Wayne believed the others were questioning my judgment for hiring such a youngster, and he says today, "I was passionate that I was not going to let Truett down." Wayne lived up to the challenge, and more than thirty years later he remains one of our top Operators.

We've hired many young Operators through the years, and a large number of those have worked within our system and met challenges as team members and team leaders. But that experience could not fully prepare them to operate a million-dollar business.

"Running the restaurant is a whole new ballgame," says Mark Reed. "The hours and the pressure are unbelievable at first. I lost twenty pounds that I didn't need to lose when I became an Operator."

But Mark had a new identity, Chick-fil-A Operator, and he was determined to live up to it. He refused to quit, even on mornings when he was so exhausted he wept in the shower. "There was no going back," he says. He

Mark had a new identity, and he was determined to live up to it.

matured quickly, learned how to delegate and train others, and after a couple of years he had his restaurant humming.

Humility

"Humility and the fear of the Lord bring wealth and honor and life" (Proverbs 22:4). Having a name to live up to means a child has acknowledged something or someone is greater than himself and has taken the first step toward humility. Christ acknowledged the importance of humility in the Sermon on the Mount by lifting up the "poor in spirit," "those who mourn," and "the meek."

My oldest son, Dan, was giving a college commencement address when he asked the graduates, "Are you ready for a life full of meaning and purpose?"

To demonstrate how they might achieve such a life, he stepped away from the microphone, got on his knees, took a shoeshine brush out of his pocket, and began to shine the shoes of the college president. Dan's point was that the strongest leaders are servants first. They humble themselves before God and other people.

He reminded the graduates that one of Jesus' last acts before His death was to kneel down and wash the feet of His disciples—at the same meal where the disciples had argued over who among them would be the greatest. They still didn't get it, so Jesus, through this act of great humility, gave those closest to Him an example of the kind of humble leadership He wanted them to demonstrate to the world.

Dan was conveying the same message to the graduates when he gave them their own shoe brushes—"leadership development tools," he called them.

Modeling Humility

You can't make a child be humble any more than you can make a child love. But you can teach humility to children by serving others and by giving children opportunities to practice humble service.

Jesus, through this act of great humility, gave those closest to Him an example of the kind of humble leadership He wanted them to demonstrate to the world.

We model humility for children through our own service. For example, Chick-fil-A restaurant Operators must demonstrate to their team members that they are willing to tackle any job in the restaurant by occasionally mopping the floors or cleaning the bathrooms—even though those jobs fall under someone else's responsibilities.

If Dan, who is now president of Chick-fil-A, sees a piece of paper in a parking lot—not just a Chick-fil-A parking lot—he picks it up and throws it away. When he's in a restaurant, he helps customers carry their trays to their tables.

A traveling companion was surprised when I took his suitcase from a baggage carousel at the airport. I wasn't trying to make a point of being humble; I was just helping a friend with his luggage.

A supervisor who models humility will accept the most menial tasks.

Likewise, at home a father should be willing to scrub the floor, do the laundry, or any other task he thinks "is not my job." In his bestselling book *Good to Great*, author Jim Collins says the leaders of America's greatest companies "channel their ego needs away from themselves and into the larger goal of building a great company. . . . Their ambition is first and foremost for the institution, not for themselves."

A parent's ambition should be not for himself but for the greatest institution in the world, the family. When our children see us serving others, they begin to understand that they also should serve.

Practicing Humility

We reinforce humility through practice. All three of

our children, Dan, Bubba, and Trudy, learned to serve while working alongside Jeannette and me at our first restaurant, the Dwarf House. It was a matter of necessity in our family business. When they were very young they dressed up like dwarfs and sang to customers while I worked behind the counter and Jeannette was at the cash register. As they grew they learned to do almost everything in the restaurant: wash dishes, serve customers, and clean up. They particularly remember scraping gum from under the counter.

They also learned that their responsibility to serve others did not end with our family or our restaurant. Jeannette often took them to a nearby nursing home, where they entertained the residents with music, short poems, or by reciting scripture.

You can give children opportunities to serve the family by performing chores whose only reward will be your gratitude. Then they can serve the community and experience the gratitude of others.

Trudy and John moved to Brazil for ten years to serve the people there as missionaries. Their children grew up serving rice and beans to neighbors who otherwise might have gone hungry. After they came home, their son John went to Auburn University, where he tried out for the football team. He made the team as a third-string kicker, which meant he dressed out for a few games, but he had little chance of actually kicking in one. Still, he had to attend every practice, hold the ball for the other kickers, then gather all the balls after practice, experiencing the satisfaction of a servant.

The Ultimate Blessing: Building and Transforming Lives

God wants to work through you to change the life of a child. Make yourself available to Him, and He may bless you with the opportunity to watch Him build and transform a life.

One of Doug and Julie Bowling's foster children wrote them a letter and followed up with a phone call apologizing for all the hardship she had brought into their home. She had been an extremely difficult teenager, and she asked them, "What can I do to make it right?"

That young lady had been transformed by God's love, expressed through Doug and Julie.

"All I ask you to do," Julie replied, "is take care of your own children. Break the cycle of abandonment that you experienced from your own parents. Let God plant a seed of love and hope in your children's hearts."

That's what God is asking you today.

"Feed My sheep."

"Do for one of the least of these."

"Welcome the little children in My name."

Let Him use you to change the life of a child, then experience the blessing of your own transformation.

TRIBUTE

I try to avoid weekend business trips so I can be in my home church on Sunday mornings teaching Sunday school. One weekend in the 1960s, however, when I had just started Chick-fil-A, a weekend trip to Houston kept me away. So I visited First Methodist Church of Houston, where Dr. Charles Allen was pastor. Jeannette and I had visited his church in Atlanta on many Sunday nights before he moved to Houston.

In the course of his sermon, Dr. Allen told of a telephone call he had received the previous week from a pastor friend back in Georgia. His friend's son had recently been arrested for an offense in Houston.

"My friend asked if I might visit his son and send word back that he was all right," Dr. Allen said. "So I went down to the jail yesterday expecting to see the son, but he had been picked up in California and was not due back here for several days."

Dr. Allen called back to Georgia on Saturday night and explained the situation to his friend and his wife. They talked for several minutes, and Dr. Allen learned that his friends hadn't heard from their son for five years. "The call from the police was the first information we've had about him since he disappeared," the Georgia pastor said.

Then the wife told Dr. Allen that every time the telephone had rung for those five years, especially at night when all was quiet, their hearts had skipped a beat because they thought it might be their son calling home.

"So, Charles," the wife said, "the next time you call, please don't call so late at night. It gets our hopes up again, and we're so disappointed when it's not him."

Sometimes, even when parents and mentors seemingly do everything right in bringing up a child, that child makes wrong choices. Ultimately, the child chooses which direction to go. I would like to offer tribute to those parents who tried to teach their children well but whose hearts were broken by the choices their children made.